W9-CHD-197

DETROIT PUBLIC LIBRARY

WILDER BRANCH LIBRARY
7140 E. SEVEN MILE RD.
DETROIT, MI 48234

DATE DUE

BC-3

AUG - - 2000

W

Your Government: How It Works

The History of Third Parties

Norma Jean Lutz

Arthur M. Schlesinger, jr.
Senior Consulting Editor

Chelsea House Publishers
Philadelphia

*Dedicated to the congenial,
friendly librarians at the
Brookside Branch in Tulsa.
Thanks!*

CHELSEA HOUSE PUBLISHERS
Editor in Chief Stephen Reginald
Production Manager Pamela Loos
Art Director Sara Davis
Director of Photography Judy L. Hasday
Managing Editor James D. Gallagher
Senior Production Editor LeeAnne Gelletly

Staff for THE HISTORY OF THIRD PARTIES
Project Editor Anne Hill
Project Editor/Publishing Coordinator Jim McAvoy
Associate Art Director Takeshi Takahashi
Series Designer Takeshi Takahashi, Keith Trego

©2000 by Chelsea House Publishers, a subsidiary of Haights Cross
Communications. All rights reserved. Printed and bound in the
United States of America.

The Chelsea House World Wide Web address is
http://www.chelseahouse.com

First Printing
1 3 5 7 9 8 6 4 2

Library of Congress Cataloging-in-Publication Data

Lutz, Norma Jean.
      The history of third parties / by Norma Jean Lutz.
          p. cm. — (Your government—how it works)
      Includes bibliographical references and index.
      Summary: Examines the participation of smaller political par-
ties in America's election process from the abolitionist Liberty
Party to the campaigns of Reform Party candidates Ross Perot
and Jesse Ventura.
      ISBN 0-7910-5541-8
      1. Third parties (United States politics)—History—Juvenile liter-
ature. 2. United States—Politics and government—Juvenile litera-
ture [1. Third parties (United States politics) 2. Political parties.
3. United States—Politics and government.] I. Title. II. Series.

JK2261 .L88 2000
324.273'09—dc21   99-048455

Contents

Introduction

Government: Crises of Confidence

Arthur M. Schlesinger, jr.

FROM THE START, Americans have regarded their government with a mixture of reliance and mistrust. The men who founded the republic understood the importance of government. "If men were angels," observed the 51st Federalist Paper, "no government would be necessary." But men are not angels. Because human beings are subject to wicked as well as to noble impulses, government was deemed essential to assure freedom and order.

The American revolutionaries, however, also knew that government could become a source of injury and oppression. The men who gathered in Philadelphia in 1787 to write the Constitution therefore had two purposes in mind: They wanted to establish a strong central authority and to limit that central authority's capacity to abuse its power.

To prevent the abuse of power, the Founding Fathers wrote two basic principles into the Constitution. The principle of federalism divided power between the state governments and the central authority. The principle of the separation of powers subdivided the central authority itself into three branches—the executive, the legislative, and the judiciary—so that "each may be a check on the other."

YOUR GOVERNMENT: HOW IT WORKS examines some of the major parts of that central authority, the federal government. It explains how various officials, agencies, and departments operate and explores the political organizations that have grown up to serve the needs of government.

Introduction

The federal government as presented in the Constitution was more an idealistic construct than a practical administrative structure. It was barely functional when it came into being.

This was especially true of the executive branch. The Constitution did not describe the executive branch in any detail. After vesting executive power in the president, it assumed the existence of "executive departments" without specifying what these departments should be. Congress began defining their functions in 1789 by creating the Departments of State, Treasury, and War.

President Washington, assisted by Secretary of the Treasury Alexander Hamilton, equipped the infant republic with a working administrative structure. Congress also continued that process by creating more executive departments as they were needed.

Throughout the 19th century, the number of federal government workers increased at a consistently faster rate than did the population. Increasing concerns about the politicization of public service led to efforts—bitterly opposed by politicians—to reform it in the latter part of the century.

The 20th century saw considerable expansion of the federal establishment. More importantly, it saw growing impatience with bureaucracy in society as a whole.

The Great Depression during the 1930s confronted the nation with its greatest crisis since the Civil War. Under Franklin Roosevelt, the New Deal reshaped the federal government, assigning it a variety of new responsibilities and greatly expanding its regulatory functions. By 1940, the number of federal workers passed the 1 million mark.

Critics complained of big government and bureaucracy. Business owners resented federal regulation. Conservatives worried about the impact of paternalistic government on self-reliance, on community responsibility, and on economic and personal freedom.

When the United States entered World War II in 1941, government agencies focused their energies on supporting the war effort. By the end of World War II, federal civilian employment had risen to 3.8 million. With peace, the federal establishment declined to around 2 million in 1950. Then growth resumed, reaching 2.8 million by the 1980s.

A large part of this growth was the result of the national government assuming new functions such as: affirmative action in civil rights, environmental protection, and safety and health in the workplace.

Some critics became convinced that the national government was a steadily growing behemoth swallowing up the liberties of the people. The 1980s brought new intensity to the debate about government growth. Foes of Washington bureaucrats preferred local government, feeling it more responsive to popular needs.

But local government is characteristically the government of the locally powerful. Historically, the locally powerless have often won their human and constitutional rights by appealing to the national government. The national government has defended racial justice against local bigotry, upheld the Bill of Rights against local vigilantism, and protected natural resources from local greed. It has civilized industry and secured the rights of labor organizations. Had the states' rights creed prevailed, perhaps slavery would still exist in the United States.

Americans are still of two minds. When pollsters ask large, spacious questions—Do you think government has become too involved in your lives? Do you think government should stop regulating business?—a sizable majority opposes big government. But when asked specific questions about the practical work of government—Do you favor Social Security? Unemployment compensation? Medicare? Health and safety standards in factories? Environmental protection?—a sizable majority approves of intervention.

We do not like bureaucracy, but we cannot live without it. We need its genius for organizing the intricate details of our daily lives. Without bureaucracy, modern society would collapse. It would be impossible to run any of the large public and private organizations we depend on without bureaucracy's division of labor and hierarchy of authority. The challenge is to keep these necessary structures of our civilization flexible, efficient, and capable of innovation.

More than 200 years after the drafting of the Constitution, Americans still rely on government but also mistrust it. These attitudes continue to serve us well. What we mistrust, we are more likely to monitor. And government needs our constant attention if it is to avoid inefficiency, incompetence, and arbitrariness. Without our informed participation, it cannot serve us individually or help us as a people to attain the lofty goals of the Founding Fathers.

Reform Party candidate Ross Perot talks with Larry King in a televised interview.

CHAPTER 1

A Billionaire for President?

TELEVISION VIEWERS WATCHING THE *Larry King Live* show on February 20, 1992, saw a man who said he wanted to become president of the United States. The man was short in stature and had big ears, a high-pitched voice, and a Texas accent. This man, whose name was Henry Ross Perot, was a very rich businessman—a billionaire. Although it was not unusual for someone to run for president, it *was* unusual not to have the backing of either of the big political parties. Ross Perot was not running as a Republican or a Democrat. He was a third-party **candidate.** In spite of the fact that there may be many political parties, the term **third party** is used to describe any party other than the Republican or Democratic parties.

Perot was born in Texarkana, Texas, in 1930. Growing up in the time of the Great Depression, he learned thriftiness and hard work. Most Boy Scouts take three to five years to earn the award of Eagle Scout. Perot achieved it in 16 months.

Entry into Business

At the age of 19, he was accepted into the U.S. Naval Academy. He was not a particularly good student, but he was well-liked. In fact, he was voted class president by his classmates. While in the Navy, he learned basic computer skills. In 1957, after leaving the Navy, these computer skills helped him get a job in Dallas at a company called International Business Machines (IBM).

His wife, Margot, taught school and Perot sold computers. Soon Perot's personable manner made him a top-notch salesman. He was bringing in more money in commissions than his bosses were earning in salaries. This caused the Dallas IBM office to set a limit on the amount of commission a salesperson could earn in a year. Perot earned that amount in three weeks. Perot was also giving the company his ideas for custom-designed computer systems, but no one listened.

In frustration, Perot quit IBM in 1962 and started his own business, Electronic Data Systems (EDS). His profits took off like a rocket. Within a few years he had become a millionaire. He gave much of his money to charitable causes.

Entry into Politics

Perot's first entry into politics was during the Vietnam war. In 1969 he spent more than a million dollars on television and newspaper ads in favor of the war. He felt the war was necessary to stop the spread of communism. Later that same year, he attempted to deliver 30 tons of food, medicine, mail, and other gifts to U.S. prisoners of war being held in Hanoi in North Vietnam. Although his efforts failed, they did cause the North Vietnamese to improve conditions for the prisoners.

In 1985 he sold his interests in his business. The profits from that sale made him a billionaire. After that time he was often urged by friends to run for president. He told them he wouldn't even run for dogcatcher. However, all that changed in 1992.

Candidate for President

On Larry King's show Perot stated that if enough people wanted him to run for president, he would. This came at a time when the American public's distrust of politicians was at an all-time high. They liked what Perot stood for. He came from a middle-class family and had worked his way up.

People also liked what Perot said. He pointed out the dangers of the nation's multitrillion dollar deficit. He promised to keep the public involved in decision making by creating an "electronic town hall." He was committed to appointing the best people for government jobs, regardless of which party they belonged to. Finally, he promised to "clean out the barn," which meant he wanted to rid the government of the layers of bureaucracy that wastes millions of taxpayer dollars. Perot viewed the present government as "broken" and he was going to fix it.

Perot's **campaign** was like nothing the nation had ever seen. Since he was using his own money, there was no limit to the amount he could spend. Some say it eventually amounted to over $60 million. The businessman made extensive use of television, featuring interviews, spot ads, and paid specials. As a third-party candidate he was even included in the fall presidential debates—something that had never happened before. By the summer of 1992, the polls showed Perot running ahead of President George Bush and the Democratic challenger, Bill Clinton.

In spite of the fact that Perot was extremely wealthy, newspapers referred to him as a populist. This meant he seemed to understand and could sympathize with the concerns of ordinary people. Problems in his campaign came

Democrat Bill Clinton (left), third-party candidate Ross Perot (center), and Republican President George Bush (right) in a televised debate. It was the first time that a third-party candidate had been invited to participate in the fall presidential debates.

when he failed to be specific about how he planned to repair the government. No clear plan was laid out. Some critics accused him of saying one thing and doing another.

Out and Back in Again

In a shocking move Perot withdrew from the race in July, leaving many saddened supporters. This strange action got him front page coverage in *Newsweek* magazine. During the week of the Republican national convention in Houston, Perot released his platform (the principles he believed in) in a book entitled, *United We Stand: How We Can Take Back Our Country.* It quickly rose to the bestseller list. In spite of the fact that Perot was out of the race, petition drives continued.

On October 1, in yet another surprise move, Perot announced he was back in the race to stay. For five weeks he made use of television interviews and call-in shows to influence voters. In the early part of the campaign, Perot strongly attacked Bush. However, as the election neared,

he came out against Clinton, questioning Clinton's ability to serve as president.

Perot chose James Stockdale, a retired Navy vice admiral, for his running mate. Stockdale had been a prisoner of war in Vietnam. Although his credentials were credible, the 68-year-old Stockdale made a poor showing in the debate with Dan Quayle and Al Gore, the running mates of the major political parties.

Retired Vice Admiral James B. Stockdale, United States Navy, Perot's running mate.

Twenty Million Votes

When election day finally arrived, Perot did not win the election, but he did attract nearly 20 million votes. This was the largest number of votes received by a third-party candidate since Theodore Roosevelt in 1912. This was a phenomenal feat because most people had never even heard of Perot before he appeared on the *Larry King Show* in February. Perot's showing was proof that most Americans were dissatisfied with what the Democrats and Republicans were doing at the time. It also proved that

Americans were looking for action rather than talk. Many have said that Perot's run for the presidency took votes from Bush, allowing Clinton to win the election.

Many of Perot's followers vowed to carry on after the election. No one was sure, however, what form the movement should take. It was hoped they could convince Perot to run again in 1996, but their efforts failed. Although Perot's movement now appears to be fading, his candidacy proved that American voters will readily turn to another party to voice their dissatisfaction.

Jesse Ventura

Further proof came about in the 1998 Minnesota gubernatorial election, when Jesse Ventura entered the race on the Reform Party ticket. Ventura had been a professional wrestler, a movie star, and a radio show host. Except for serving as mayor of Brooklyn Park, Minnesota, Ventura

Minnesota governor-elect Jesse Ventura answers questions in front of the Capitol building after the November 1998 election.

knew little about politics. At first no one took him seriously, but his popularity grew. In the November election, he beat out two career politicians, making him the first Reform Party member to win a statewide office.

Perot and Ventura are only two of the most recent in a long list of persons to run for political office outside the ranks of the two major political parties.

Summary

America's politics has been run by a two-party system ever since 1854. In spite of the fact that the Republicans and the Democrats are supposed to be opposing forces, voters often feel the two are so much alike that it amounts to no real choice at all. As a result, hundreds of political parties have sprung up throughout our history. More than 100 third-party candidates have tried to win votes in presidential elections. Some have been strong enough to have their name appear on a national ballot.

Although they realize they have little chance of winning, these third-party groups and their candidates have affected America's political structure and have changed the course of history.

*The Thomas Jefferson
Memorial, Washington, D.C.
Jefferson, the leader of one of
the first two political factions in
American politics, wanted to
return government to the people.*

Special Place for Third Parties

DURING THE REVOLUTIONARY WAR, the patriots who fought for independence were drawn together in unity. The patriots, often referred to as Whigs, were fighting against the colonials, called Tories, who were loyal to the British Crown. Even as the Constitution was being drafted in Philadelphia during the summer of 1787, the Founding Fathers never imagined that there might be opposing political parties. President George Washington, especially, was against political **factions.** However, a young nation filled with people of different backgrounds could not be expected to agree on all government matters.

Once the national government was established by the Constitution, it followed that the leadership of such a government was a prize worth fighting for. The actions of the government would affect all the people of the nation, and the leadership of one group might work against the interests of another. This need for representation is what led to the creation of political parties.

Alexander Hamilton,
first secretary of the
United States Treasury,
was also the leader of
the Federalist faction.

Alexander Hamilton, first secretary of the United States Treasury, was also the leader of the Federalist faction.

The First Factions

The first two factions in American government were sitting right there in President Washington's cabinet. Alexander Hamilton, secretary of the treasury, was a wealthy man who believed government should be conducted in a court system patterned after the British monarchy.

Thomas Jefferson, secretary of state, grew up in Virginia, which was at that time the edge of the American frontier. He believed in the rights of man and felt that men should decide their own destiny with little interference from the government. President Washington was greatly distressed over the conflict between these two men.

Hamilton's method was to act like a dictator and steamroll his bills through Congress. He was the hero of men of power and wealth. At that time only wealthy landowners had the right to vote. These Federalists, as they were called, were soon hated by the ordinary people who were denied the right to have a say.

Jefferson contrived the idea to draw leaders and groups into one national party. He wanted the local leaders in each state to organize and rally their followers. The plan was to oust the Federalists and return government to the people. The battle became vicious as Jefferson turned to the newspapers to lay his case before the people—much as political opponents do today.

Establishment of the Two-Party System

Jefferson was eventually able to put together a political party; and in the election of 1800, he defeated the Federalists and became president. In the process, the two-party system was established. By 1840 most Americans thought of themselves as either a Whig or a Democrat in both state and national elections.

Through the years this system has seen only a few changes as it transformed slowly into the two major parties that we know today. From 1856 to the present day, every president has been either a Democrat or a Republican. Amazing as it may appear to other nations, once a party wins the election, the opposing party sets about to support the party in power. Never has one group violently moved to take over the other.

Emergence of Third Parties

To most Americans, the Democratic and Republican parties are as much a part of the American culture as the Stars and Stripes. There have been times, however, when the people felt that neither party represented them well. When this happened, small minority groups emerged as a way to offer yet another choice.

People who undertake such a course of action do so because they feel something is wrong with "politics as

Campaign button for Theodore Roosevelt's Progressive or "Bull Moose" party, 1912.

usual." They are determined to make things right, in spite of the fact that they must face overwhelming odds. It has never been easy to be a part of a third party, nor is it easy to vote for a third-party candidate (a person seeking an office). Political leaders who leave one of the two major parties may lose their good standing. Most candidates will attempt other methods of making their voices heard. They take the third-party route only as a last resort.

Third parties usually emerge in one of three ways. First, a group may break away from the existing major party. This happened with the Southern Democrats in 1859 when they broke away from the Democratic party. Second, a third party may rise up independent of either party. This happened in 1892 when the People's party, made up of western farmers, felt they were not represented fairly in the nation's government. Third, a party may form behind the leadership of one person. This happened when a furious Theodore Roosevelt walked away from the Republican party in 1912. The group that followed him was called the Progressive party.

Third-Party Hurdles

Ballot Access Restrictions   Once a party decides to run a candidate for the presidency, they face a number of monumental hurdles, the biggest of which is ballot access restrictions. In the years before 1890, the ballots (or tickets, as they were called) were printed and distributed by the political parties rather than by the states. These ballots were of a distinct color and shape. Voters walked into the polling place, chose a ticket, and dropped it in the ballot box. Unless the voter scratched off a name or wrote in a name, he was forced to vote for the entire **party slate.** (Only men could vote before 1920.)

In one respect it was simple for third-party candidates to print their own ballots. The disadvantage was that the voter had to abandon his party for every office that was at stake. Another disadvantage lay in the fact that voting was a public act, and the cost of betraying the existing party was high. Added to that was the problem of raising money and organizing enough workers to print and distribute ballots in every voting place in the nation.

Later the states prepared official ballots listing all the party slates; and voters marked them secretly. However, the question came up of who should be listed on the official ballot. Laws emerged that made it difficult for third-party candidates to get on the ballot.

Because each state determines its own ballot access laws, there are dozens of different sets of rules with which to comply. Third-party candidates must circulate petitions within a particular time frame. Filing deadlines also vary. Some deadlines are early in the election cycle, some are much later. Consequently, a third-party candidate cannot mount a nationwide effort; instead, he or she must hold 51 different drives at different times. (One for every state and one for the District of Columbia.)

Petition Signatures The number of signatures needed on a petition differs from state to state. A candidate may need to gather millions of signatures in order to comply with the rules and regulations. In some states those who sign a third-party petition become ineligible to vote in the primary election. Other states require that signatures be certified. These rules work to discourage voters from signing petitions in support of a third-party candidate.

Many of these restrictions came into being during the two world wars when suspicion and distrust ran high. Stringent rules were in place to prevent a possible government takeover. Recent court decisions have made ballot access laws more lenient. Still, it is a difficult task for any third-party candidate to obtain a position on the ballot.

Finance Laws   Yet another hurdle in the election process is the finance laws. In 1974 the Federal Election Campaign Act (FECA) adopted a new law that provides a lump sum of money for major party **nominees.** This is not the case for third-party candidates. They are not eligible for public funds until *after* the election and then only if they meet a number of requirements. Very few have ever met these requirements.

Press Coverage   Third parties usually receive poorer press coverage. The media are either hostile toward them or will ignore them altogether. Although some third-party groups may have their own newspapers to reach the public, they still have difficulty reaching and pulling in new supporters.

Lack of Recognition   Third-party candidates are often unknown and unqualified. When supporting a nominee for president, voters look for political experience such as the holding of a high office (governor, U.S. senator, or U.S. representative). The majority of major party presidential nominees have held such posts; few third-party candidates have ever held these positions.

Voter Beliefs   Another problem that third-party candidates face is the mind-set of the American public. History shows that most third-party candidates begin with a flurry of support. As election time draws near, however, the support dwindles. This is because the public knows the candidate will not win, so why should they "waste" their vote? Another belief is that the two-party system is the "American way." Very few people want to change that system.

Undermining by Major Parties As if these obstacles were not enough, the major parties work hard to undermine any third-party position that appears to be a threat. The new **party platform** may showcase an important vision or center on a controversial issue. When the major parties see that the issue is important to the people, one or the other may take up the vision as its own. For instance, before Perot began his campaign, neither party was paying much attention to the issues of the national debt. After he came back into the race in October, he hammered away at the subject of debt reduction. It quickly turned into one of the more important issues.

Summary

In spite of the challenges listed here, third parties continue to make a strong showing, as in the case of Ross Perot. Some third-party candidates have even claimed enough votes to change an election. When former president Theodore Roosevelt ran as a Progressive in 1912, he took enough votes away from William Howard Taft to allow Woodrow Wilson to be elected.

Through the years, third parties have offered refuge for disgruntled voters. They offer a place where important issues can be addressed—issues that might be too controversial for the major parties to handle. New ideas are introduced through third-party groups and are then presented to the public. In addition, as most Americans will admit, third parties can liven up an otherwise dull political race.

135,000 SETS, 270,000 VOLUMES SOLD.

UNCLE TOM'S CABIN

FOR SALE HERE.

AN EDITION FOR THE MILLION, COMPLETE IN 1 Vol., PRICE 37 1-2 CENTS.
"   "   IN GERMAN, IN 1 Vol., PRICE 50 CENTS.
"   "   IN 2 Vols,. CLOTH, 6 PLATES, PRICE $1.50.
SUPERB ILLUSTRATED EDITION, IN 1 Vol., WITH 153 ENGRAVINGS,
PRICES FROM $2.50 TO $5.00.

The Greatest Book of the Age.

Abolitionists before the Civil War were divided about how they thought slavery should be ended. Harriet Beecher Stowe's novel Uncle Tom's Cabin *helped to unite the North and strengthen its determination to take action.*

CHAPTER 3

Third Parties Before the Civil War

THE ISSUE OF SLAVERY had been a subject of debate in the United States since colonial times. By the early 1800s the controversy had become more vocal and more complex. The practice of owning slaves and using them for labor had created a huge economic base in the Southern states. Thousands of large plantations became wealthy thanks to free slave labor. Slaveholders believed it was the right of the individual states to decide if they could own slaves. It was in their interest to see to it that new territories joining the Union become slave states.

Abolitionists

Abolitionists, however, strongly disagreed. They wanted all new territories to be free. These disagreements spilled over into the political arena, bringing deep divisions and creating a new crop of third parties.

In the 1830s a number of groups, called societies, were formed with the goal of abolishing slavery in the United States. The problem was that none of them could agree on how this abolition should be carried out. Some groups wanted the spread of slavery stopped; others wanted slavery abolished everywhere. Some groups felt they needed to organize a political party; others felt slavery was more a moral issue than a political one. Even those abolitionists who believed slavery was a political issue did not agree that a third party should be formed. Many felt it was best to work within their own party, whether Whig or Democrat.

Liberty Party

The American Antislavery Society came together in 1839 to discuss forming a separate political party, but it was never brought to a vote. Out of this group came another nominating convention, which met in Albany, New York, in April of 1840. The members of the group nominated James Birney as their candidate for the presidency, and named their party the Liberty party. One single plank made up their platform—that of antislavery.

Theirs was more of a move of protest than a political move. They were poorly organized, and they had a difficult time convincing Whig abolitionists to cast a vote for such a weak party. Most voters were more concerned with issues such as banking and tariffs to pay much attention to slavery.

When election day came, there were too few Liberty ballots printed, and some locales had none at all. This cut into the few votes they were able to claim. In spite of their weak showing nationally, the Liberty party eventually began to do well locally. The votes they did receive usually came from the Whig party.

By the election year of 1844, slavery issues were splitting the two major parties. The two candidates were slaveowners, James K. Polk and Henry Clay. The Whigs warned voters to stay with the party because giving their votes to

Henry Clay, shown here addressing the United States Senate, was the Whig candidate in the 1844 election. Salmon P. Chase is seated in the first row, far left, behind Clay.

the Liberty party could throw the election to Democrat Polk—whom they accused of being even more proslavery than Clay.

James Birney was again the Liberty candidate and he made a better showing than in 1840. However, by 1847, the strength of the Liberty party was waning.

Free-Soil Group

An attorney from Cincinnati, Salmon Portland Chase, was an ardent abolitionist. He believed that black people had the right to vote and to an education and that they should be able to testify in court against white people. These beliefs made him very unpopular with most white people. When an angry mob tried to shut down an abolitionist newspaper, Attorney Chase defended the owner.

Because Cincinnati was situated directly across the Ohio River from Kentucky—a slave state—many slaves used the river as a means of escape. Soon Chase found himself defending runaway slaves both in local and federal court. He was called the Attorney General of Fugitive Slaves.

Chase became active in the Liberty party, urging party members to select more prominent nominees (people chosen as candidates for an election). Later he encouraged the leaders to broaden their platform and to join with other antislavery groups. Chase and other leaders of the Liberty party joined with a group known as the Free-Soil group at their **political convention** in Albany in 1848. Their slogan was "Free Men, Free Soil, and Free Trade." Other groups, such as the Barnburners, and the Hunkers joined this convention, making it broader-based than before.

Chase wrote much of the platform for this convention. The platform called for an end to slavery in the territories and a ban on adding any new slave states to the Union. Former President Martin Van Buren became the nominee for president. Although he made a very weak showing, the Free-Soil party still managed to elect nine congressional representatives.

Eventually the crisis over slavery became so heated, it was beyond the resources of a small third party. Free-Soil men would eventually flock to the new Republican party in 1854. Meanwhile, these small third-party groups had succeeded in drawing the nation's attention to the issue of slavery.

Southern Democrats

Abolitionists felt they needed a third party to air their views. In contrast, proslavery forces remained comfortable within the ranks of the major parties—until 1860, that is. Most Southern Democrats cared little about party unity; their main goal was the defense of slavery.

Slaveholders had received support from the Supreme Court *Dred Scott* decision, which said that a black person had no standing in a court of law to sue. Prior to the *Dred Scott* decision, the U.S. Constitution may have tolerated but did not protect slavery. After this landmark decision, the Constitution did indeed protect slavery. This was what the slaveholders needed to strengthen their position. Their goal was to promote a slave code that would protect slavery in the territories.

Dred Scott. The 1857
Dred Scott *decision,*
which protected slavery
under the Constitution,
encouraged Southern
Democrats to seek
protection for slavery in
the territories.

When this code was not accepted at the 1860 Democratic convention, delegates from nine Southern states walked out in protest. This left the Democratic party split in two. These Southern delegates held their own convention and nominated Vice President John C. Breckinridge. (He later became the secretary of war of the Confederacy.) This split weakened the Democratic party, opening the way for the Republican candidate, Abraham Lincoln, to win the election.

The Southern Democrats were a type of third party. In a stricter sense, however, they were secessionists, which meant they were ready to be the primary party of a new nation: the Confederate States of America. Within a year, the Civil War was under way.

Nativists

Yet another problem that arose during the 1840s and 1850s was that of record numbers of immigrants coming to this country. Many American resented this flood of newcomers. Organizations formed that were based on fear and distrust of foreigners. An intense hatred for Catholics was also a basis for the unity of these groups, who were called Nativists. (They considered themselves to be the natives of the land.)

Thousands of immigrants who had come mostly from Germany and Ireland became part of the Democratic political machines. Non-Democratic, old-stock Americans believed that Europe was purposely dumping unproductive citizens on America's shores to weaken the United States. They also felt that immigrants were taking all the jobs and keeping wages low. Because most immigrants were members of the Democratic party, the nativists believe immigrants gave too much power to that major party.

The American party began as an anti-Catholic and anti-immigrant association. The members demanded restrictions on immigration laws and set about to make life difficult for new immigrants. The workings of the American party were highly secretive. When asked about the party, members answered, "I know nothing." This is why Horace Greeley, editor of the *New York Tribune,* called them Know-Nothings.

The Know-Nothing victories in state and local election took the country by surprise. By 1854 they controlled the legislatures of several states. Three years later they controlled six state governorships. Their share of seats in Congress was larger than that of any other third party in history. Nathaniel Banks of the American party was the only third-party House member ever to become House Speaker.

In spite of the strong presence in Congress, the Nativists were never able to fully enact their immigration reforms. These reforms would have included a proposal for a 21-year naturalization period and a ban on all "foreign paupers, criminals, idiots, lunatics, insane, and blind persons."

Horace Greeley, editor of the New York Tribune, *used the name "Know-Nothings" to describe the American party.*

Interestingly, the American party brought about reform for the working class in the state of Massachusetts. They were able to abolish imprisonment for debt, and they instituted the early safety measures for railroad crossings.

As with most all other political parties during this time, the American party became divided over slavery issues. The Southern segment of the party nominated Millard Fillmore at the 1856 convention. This was a departure from their anti-Catholic stand because Fillmore had an audience with the Pope upon his selection. The Northern Nativists became more vocal against slavery than they ever had against immigration. Eventually they cast their lot in with the newly formed Republican party.

Summary

During the Civil War, third parties faded from view. Rather than splinter groups forming, the nation was divided against itself, the North against the South. Whether they were for the Union or for the Confederacy, Americans were focused solely on the war efforts.

Construction workers melting metal. Because there was no public relief available at the time of the depression, new third parties were formed to represent destitute farmers and out-of-work laborers.

CHAPTER **4**

Third Parties Following the Civil War

IN THE LATTER DECADES of the 1800s, the main driving force behind third parties had to do with labor, social issues, and the monetary system. **Monopolies** were creating unimaginable wealth, and yet laborers in factories were receiving paupers' wages. Some stated that the Civil War had moved the country from the labor of slaves to slave wages. These conditions gave rise to different types of protest parties.

Farmers, too, were having a difficult time. Prosperous years of plenty soon turned to drought and plagues of grasshoppers. Many had borrowed on credit in order to purchase their farms. Being deeply in debt made the hard times doubly hard.

Farmers were also victims of high railroad freight rates and high rates charged by grain elevators. In protest, they launched a fraternal order, the Patrons of Husbandry, also called the Grange. (In later years, Grange halls became places for rural social gatherings.) Grangers in many states formed an alliance with Democrats, attacking banking, railroad, manufacturing, land, and grain monopolies.

Prices fell during the Panic of 1873, causing many farmers to go bankrupt or lose their farms. What followed was an industrial depression with falling stock market prices, bank failures, and plant shutdowns. The stock market actually came to a halt for ten days. There was no such thing as public relief in those days. Long bread lines appeared in the cities and tramps, or hoboes, roamed the countryside.

Greenbacks

During this depression, Grange-based third-party movements formed at the state level. These included the Independent party, the National Reform party, the People's party, and the Antimonopolist Reform party. The granger campaign and the industrial depression raised the need for a new party to represent destitute farmers and out-of-work laborers. This new party was the National party, but everyone knew them as the Greenbackers.

During the Civil War the government issued paper money (greenbacks) not backed by gold or silver. After the war the government eliminated the greenbacks and returned to hard money. Greenbackers demanded an unlimited circulation of greenbacks, thinking this would help ease the country's financial woes. The Greenback party was the first to bring farmers and industrial workers together.

In 1876 the first National Greenback party held a convention and nominated Peter Cooper of New York as their choice for president. He drew very few votes, but the party was making headway. Their numbers swelled because of the continuing depression. By the midterm elections they had attracted more than a million voters and captured 14 congressional seats.

This growth was due in part to the labor reformers in the group. The proposed labor reforms were new at that time but are standard now. They included child labor laws, women's **suffrage,** and a shorter work week.

As the depression ended (the Republican party claimed they were the ones who ended it), the labor-farmer coalition weakened. With the renewal of industrial activity, the farmers went back to their quarrels with the railroad, and the laborers went back to their quarrels with employers. In its place a new Anti-Monopoly party had taken on the reforms of the Greenbacks. When the Governor of Massachusetts, Benjamin Butler, became the Greenback's candidate for president in 1884, he encouraged the smaller groups to unite into the People's party.

The third-party movements of the 1870s and 1880s may have failed to make major strides in national elections, but they did make inroads in state and local elections. They continued to hope that they would come up with the just-right combination to bring a new party into power. It looked as if the People's party (the Populists) might be that party.

Farmers faced great hardships during the decades after the Civil War. Many united to form the Patrons of Husbandry, or the Grange, to protest the policies of the great railroad, land, and grain monopolies.

Populists

Farmers in the Southern states were also in dire straits after the Civil War, although their plight was different from that of the western farmers. The banking system had collapsed throughout the South and there was very little money. Southern farmers were forced to turn to merchants for help. The merchants advanced goods on a promise to receive money when the crops came in. This gave the merchants control. They hiked up the prices, then told the farmers what they could buy and how much. If the farmers' crops failed to cancel the debt, which was usually the case, they remained in bondage to the merchant for yet another year.

At the same time prices of farm goods (commodities) were falling. Most farmers believed that bankers conspired to manipulate money supplies and make money scarce. Farmers saw the expansion of money supply as the solution to the problem. Many farm organizations expounded this opinion. Founded in 1880, the Northern Alliance began in Kansas, Nebraska, Iowa, and Minnesota, the states hit hardest by the drought.

The Southern Alliance, which began in Texas to help the ranchers, merged with the Louisiana Farmers' Union in 1887. Soon the Southern Alliance had swelled to a million members. The group in the North had nearly 200,000 members. Because they were split in two, neither alliance could enact needed legislation to help its cause. The Southern group continued to work with the local Democratic party. The members took a few years before they decided that a third party would be more effective. Activities in Kansas pointed the way.

A group known as the Populists won control of the Kansas state legislature in 1890. Kansas resident William Peffer became the party's first U.S. senator. This move led to the merger of the north and the south farm alliances.

The Populists held their first convention in 1892. The national party was a **fusion** of the Farmers' Alliance and the Knights of Labor. Their presidential candidate, James

B. Weaver, won over one million votes. Populist state parties did well in many midwestern and western states. When the mid-term elections came in 1896, there were 22 Populists in Congress. In the next few years, however, Southern Democrats weakened the Populist party through fraud, intimidation, and violence.

Soon the Populists themselves were again divided. One group felt it was necessary to fuse with the Democrats. The second faction wanted to remain in the middle of the road, not fusing with either major party. This division worked to weaken the party.

One of the planks in the platform of the Populist party was a call for the coinage of silver. Another bank panic, which came along in 1893, drained the country's gold reserves. The Populists saw free silver as the answer to this problem. However, by the time their national convention was held in 1896, the Democrats had already nominated William Jennings Bryan who was running on a free-silver platform. Once again a major party had taken on the platform of a third party, thereby taking the wind out of the third-party's sails.

By the turn of the century, the Populists had slowly died away. They ran candidates in 1904 and 1908, but the votes were few. Nevertheless, their effect as a movement was strongly felt. Most of the issues of the Populist party eventually became law. In later years Theodore Roosevelt would pick up many of the planks of the Populists' platform and recast them in a new form.

Prohibition Party

The Prohibition party is best known for its desire to ban the sale, manufacture, transportation, importation, or exportation of intoxicating liquors. Although it never became a strong-running party, it can claim to be the longest-running third party in the nation. Begun in 1869, the Prohibitionists first sought to bring about an evangelistic transformation, creating a higher order in America.

In the formative years the Prohibitionists often crossed paths with the Abolitionists, sometimes supporting the same local candidates. They also sided with the Know-Nothings against Irish and German immigrants who opposed temperance.

Another group with whom the Prohibitionists were closely connected was the suffrage movement. In 1869, fully half a century before women were allowed to vote, the Prohibition Party granted equal status to women convention delegates. For years they endorsed women's suffrage (the right to vote). The Woman's Christian Temperance Union, first organized in 1874, became the women's arm of the Prohibition party.

Under the powerful leadership of Frances Willard, the WCTU outgrew the parent party. It became the largest women's organization of the 19th century. They branched out from women's suffrage and prohibition to embrace prison and labor reform, public support for neglected children, and a society dedicated to social justice.

Woman's Temperance Crusade, 1874. The Woman's Christian Temperance Union was founded based on the success of this Midwest campaign for abstinence from alcohol.

Following the Civil War, with the slavery issue settled, the Prohibition party members felt they could devote more attention to the issue of prohibition. Their cause was especially revived during the Whiskey Ring frauds under the administration of President Ulysses Grant. Secretary of the Treasury Benjamin Bristow was successful in uncovering the nationwide cover-up involving the theft of liquor tax money. Eventually, arrests of those involved in the crime ring were made in nearly every major city in the country.

In spite of the growing interest in the banning of liquor, many in the group didn't agree that politics was the best way to address this moral issue. Still others kept hoping that the Republican party would take up the cause just as it had with abolition.

During the 1870s the party's power dwindled. The liquor industry's political influence grew, and states that once had prohibition laws, moved to repeal them. At first the two major parties took steps to make concessions to appease the Prohibitionists. They soon learned, however, that the group was small and weak. More powerful were the large groups of immigrant drinkers. Theirs was the voice that moved the major parties.

The subject of free silver worked to split the Prohibition party in 1892. When the party leaders refused to add the free-silver plank to their platform, many of their number broke away in protest and formed the National party.

After the turn of the century, the Anti-Saloon League began an all-out effort to bring about prohibition. Unlike the Prohibition party, which supported a number of planks in its platform, the league was single-minded. The league remained within the major parties and did its work there. Individual candidates were considered more important than parties. The league, more than any other factor, brought about the decline of the Prohibition party. The Eighteenth Amendment in 1920 instituted nationwide prohibition. That which the party had advocated for decades was now a law.

Federal agents, enforcing the Eighteenth Amendment, recover smuggled liquor from a sunken rumrunner in 1924.

Even after prohibition became law, the party continued in spite of its small numbers. In 1933 the Eighteenth Amendment was repealed. Liquor was once again legal; and although the party was still in existence at that time, it brought no flood of voters into the ranks.

The Prohibition party continued to run candidates in every election. Earl Dodge, their candidate in the 1992 election, received only 691 votes.

The party still exists and will hold its 1999 nominating convention in Lancaster, Pennsylvania. Its platform continues to urge the repeal of all laws legalizing liquor. It also supports other conservative issues. Historical collections of books, records, and papers are maintained by the party in Denver, Colorado, and at the University of Michigan.

Summary

Third parties during the 1800s were closely linked to the major parties. They ran candidates for lower offices, held conventions to select nominees, and took a stand on a wide range of issues. They pursued the third-party route only as a last resort. The parties formed first, then the candidates were chosen—most of whom were relatively unknown. However, had these parties worked in a system with fewer restraints, they might very well have achieved the status of a major party.

European immigrants such as these, who were accustomed to socialism in their homelands, fueled the rise of the Socialist party in early 20th-century America.

CHAPTER 5

The Rise of Independents

THIRD-PARTY POLITICS UNDERWENT a noticeable change with the coming of a new century. This era saw the rise of independent campaigns as opposed to the formation of a strong group. Third parties didn't stay around long because of the lack of a substantial foundation. With the coming of radio and television, technology replaced organization as the needed ingredient for the splinter groups. The parties in the 20th century relied less and less on formal party structure.

Teddy Roosevelt

In 1900 Theodore Roosevelt won the vice presidency under William McKinley. On September 14, 1901, McKinley was killed by an assassin's bullet and Roosevelt became president. The American people loved their new president. He was the first president to stand up against big business and enforce the Sherman Anti-Trust Act. He was nicknamed the trust-buster.

When Roosevelt turned over the presidency to William Howard Taft in 1909, he was confident Taft would carry on these principles. When Taft failed to do this, Roosevelt felt that Taft had betrayed the cause by siding with big business. More than that, Roosevelt believed Taft had weakened the Republican party.

When Roosevelt returned from an African big-game safari in 1912, he carefully assessed these problems. In his mind he was the one to fix them all. He immediately threw his hat in the ring with the Republicans. At this time only a few states held primaries where voters could express their preference for their candidate. Roosevelt won the majority of these primaries. The people clearly showed that they wanted Teddy Roosevelt back in the White House.

However, in the early 1900s the selection of most delegates (and the presidential nomination) was decided by the major party leaders. Breaking away from the wishes of the people, the Republican party was determined to stay with Taft. As soon as Taft was nominated, Roosevelt supporters walked out of the convention in protest and nominated the former president as their own candidate.

When Roosevelt showed up to accept the nomination, he told the crowd he felt as fit as a bull moose. The party was quickly nicknamed the Bull Moose Progressives. Roosevelt campaigned on a platform of regulating big business, women's suffrage, a graduated income tax, and the completion of the Panama Canal.

The Democrats sized up the Republican split and chose Woodrow Wilson as their candidate. With this plan they hoped to grab the votes of the reform-minded Democrats who just might vote for Roosevelt. The plan worked.

In the November elections, Roosevelt finished with 88 electoral votes. Wilson won with 435, and Taft came through with only 8. The split in the Republican party simply paved the way for the Democrat Wilson to be elected.

LaFollette Progressive

Roosevelt wasn't the only politician upset with Taft in 1912. Robert LaFollette, a trial lawyer from Wisconsin, also ran in the Republican primaries. In 1900 LaFollette, as governor of his state, had put through laws to allow direct primaries to choose candidates for state office. LaFollette was unhappy with what he saw going on in the nation. The wealthy people used laws to avoid taxes, and poor working folk suffered under increasing tax burdens. He saw owners of big businesses gaining wealth and giving nothing back to their workers or to the community.

LaFollette was later elected a U.S. senator during Taft's term. He fought against the moneyed industrial capitalists and the influential political party bosses. When the conservative Republicans saw the problems Taft was causing, they turned to "Fighting Bob" LaFollette to take up their cause.

During World War I, LaFollette was an outspoken opponent of the fighting in Europe. Following the war he was reelected to the Senate and continued his fight against monopolies and in favor of labor and agriculture.

In 1922 several groups came together to form the Conference for Progressive Political Action. The CPPA sent several candidates to Congress that year. In the national election of 1924, they nominated LaFollette as their presidential candidate. The American Federation of Labor also supported the Wisconsin Senator, marking the first time in history that a labor organization had ever backed a presidential candidate.

Another group, called the Socialists, had joined the CPPA and went on to accept candidate LaFollette and his platform as its own. The Socialists were critical of how the campaign was run because they felt it was important to build a formal party organization to make the future secure. The labor people, in contrast, could not see past an immediate victory. They had no interest in an organized party.

It was a lonely campaign—underfinanced and almost hopeless against the popular Coolidge. Much of the campaign money promised by labor never materialized.

Despite great odds, LaFollette captured nearly five million votes. He easily won his home state of Wisconsin and ran well in the western states. Had he been elected, he would not have been in office long. Following the exhausting work of campaigning LaFollette's heart gave out, and he died in June, 1925. The CPPA held a meeting following the elections, which ended in total disagreement. The group disbanded forever.

Socialists

Most third parties stem from the two major parties, but the Socialist party was founded on ideals separate and apart from the existing parties. Different types of socialist movements had been in existence since the mid-1800s. Socialists saw government ownership of factories and utilities as the answer to the nation's economic woes.

Eugene Victor Debs eventually became the standard-bearer for this political group. Debs started off in local politics in Indiana but then turned to working with a local railroad labor union—the Brotherhood of Locomotive Firemen. Eventually he became head of a national industrial union open to all railroad employees.

Debs spent time in prison for contempt of court during a strike. While there he studied books and materials that turned him to socialism. Debs became the presidential candidate for the Socialist party for five consecutive elections. His magazine, *Appeal to Reason,* was used to tout his views. The magazine eventually reached more than two million readers.

In 1901 the Socialist party merged with the Social Laborites and the Social Democratic party. The party's strength peaked in 1912 when Debs was able to take six percent of the votes for president. That year the party

Eugene V. Debs, American Socialist party leader.

elected more than a thousand local officials and many city mayors. Twenty Socialists sat in the legislatures of six states.

The party stood against the nation's involvement in World War I. This angered many Americans. Bands of vigilantes attacked local Socialist candidates and many Socialist groups were shut down and run out of town. Debs himself landed in prison under the Espionage Act. He was sentenced to 10 years in the Atlanta penitentiary. As an inmate, he ran for president in 1920 and received more than 900,000 votes. Following the war, the weakened party joined forces with Robert LaFollette in the election of 1924.

Several causes that Debs supported, such as women's rights and government protection of workers, eventually became law. The strength of the party was greatly weakened when Debs died in 1926.

The Union Party

The misery that spread through the nation during the Great Depression caused some to be disillusioned with the governmental system. Many radicals came to the forefront, all with their own ideas of how the problem should be fixed.

Father Charles E. Coughlin, a Roman Catholic priest, became a powerful voice over the radio airwaves. A nationwide hookup brought his radio messages to 40 million Americans every week. As his power and influence grew, he became more political. He attacked capitalism, communism, socialism, and dictatorship. He spoke for democracy, but he never clearly defined what he meant by the term. Coughlin, in the early years, was friends with President Franklin D. Roosevelt and even ate at the White House. However, he later turned his attacks on the popular president. Some said it was because FDR refused to involve Coughlin in the decision making process.

At the same time, William Lemke, a Republican congressman from North Dakota, was also disgruntled with the president. Lemke had campaigned for FDR and then expected the president to support farm legislation, which Lemke was pushing through Congress. When the president failed to do so, Lemke became bitter. He saw a third-party run for the presidency as a way to get even; but he needed help. He turned to Father Coughlin.

On June 19, 1936, Coughlin announced to his listeners that he was launching the Union party. Lemke was to be the presidential candidate. This strange party attracted other radicals—none of whom trusted one other. Lemke

Food lines in 1925. Disillusionment with government caused more radical voices to be widely heard.

found to his dismay that he had very little support as he set out on the campaign trail. In order to counter the threat from the Union party, Roosevelt strengthened the Democratic platform's farm plank and then directly appealed to farmers in his campaign speeches.

Roosevelt's popularity proved to be greater than ever, which embittered Father Coughlin even more. Coughlin stated that since his followers showed no loyalty, he was dissolving the party. Lemke, who at first attempted to keep the party together for future elections, also chose to disband the Union party.

Summary

Although there was a period of unusual political turmoil before World War II, most voters still chose to cast their ballots in favor of the two major parties. The third parties were there, but they made little headway. As happened during the Civil War era, few third parties emerged during the five long years of World War II. America's focus was on the unified war efforts.

George Wallace's defiance of efforts to integrate the University of Alabama gained him enough national attention to become a third-party candidate in the 1964 presidential election.

CHAPTER **6**

Third Parties Following the War

JUST AS SLAVERY HAD affected politics before the Civil War, race relations strongly affected politics after World War II. Two other issues that gave rise to independents during this time were foreign policy issues and general disillusionment with current leadership.

The Wallace Progressives

Following the war, the party name of "progressive" surfaced once again. It was brought to light by a politician named Henry A. Wallace. Wallace had served as secretary of agriculture, then as vice president under Franklin Roosevelt. Democratic party leaders did not care for the outspoken, liberal Wallace. In the 1944 election Southern Democrats moved to have Wallace dropped from the ticket as vice president. In spite of this seeming betrayal, Wallace continued to campaign for Roosevelt. In return, Roosevelt offered him another cabinet post. Wallace chose to be secretary of commerce. (Had Wallace been retained as vice president, he rather than Harry Truman would have become president when Roosevelt died in 1945.)

When Truman became president, he allowed Wallace to remain on staff in spite of their disagreements. Wallace opposed Truman's warlike position with the Soviet Union. He feared that Truman was taking the country back to the brink of war. Wallace believed that if America stopped the arms buildup and extended peace to the Soviet Union, the Soviet Union would follow suit.

In 1946 Wallace spoke out against Truman's foreign policy in a speech in New York City. Within a week Wallace had left his position on the Truman cabinet. Some say he quit; others say Truman fired him.

Believing that it was up to him to turn the country around, Wallace organized a new Progressive party. The party was better funded than most third parties because of the backing of a number of wealthy liberals. Truman fought the threat by advocating many of the liberal domes-

Henry Wallace helped launch a new Progressive party in 1948, which opposed President Truman's hard-line policy toward the Soviet Union.

tic policies that were planks in the Progressive party's platform. He even sent Supreme Court Chief Justice Vinson to Moscow to search for ways to end the Cold War.

When Wallace accepted backing from the American Communist party, he greatly weakened his stand. Most Americans during this time associated communism with the powerful Soviet dictator Joseph Stalin. The media attacked Wallace, accusing him of following the communists too closely. Support dwindled. His threat to Truman was minimal because his showing in November was less than 1.2 million votes.

Wallace's party was the first third party to protest foreign policy. His soft line with the communists came at a time when most Americans feared them as dreaded enemies. Eventually, the Iron Curtain did disintegrate, just as Wallace had predicted it would.

The Dixiecrats

The Wallace Progressive party was not the only threat Truman faced in 1948. There was yet another, stronger, third-party group, called the Dixiecrats.

The Berlin Wall before its dismantling in 1989. It formed a border between East and West Germany and was part of the Iron Curtain, or areas of Europe controlled by the Soviet Union.

After the Progressives held their convention in Chicago, Truman set about creating a new civil rights program to provide better treatment of blacks. His plan was to abolish poll taxes and to make lynching and segregation illegal. (Poll taxes had been used for many years to prevent blacks from voting.) Truman thought this move would pull back liberal Democrats who might follow Wallace. Instead it drove away Southern Democrats who believed in states' rights and white supremacy.

When the platform was introduced at the Democratic convention, all the delegates from Mississippi walked out, along with half the delegates from Alabama. A few days later a meeting was held in Birmingham, Alabama, bringing together Southern politicians who were opposed to Truman's civil rights program. They set about to formulate a third party and run their own candidate. Because they didn't want to move too far from their parent party, they called themselves States' Rights Democrats.

For their candidates they chose Governor J. Strom Thurmond of South Carolina for president, and Governor Fielding Wright of Mississippi for vice president.

Governor J. Strom Thurmond of South Carolina was the presidential candidate of the third-party States' Rights Democrats in 1948.

The Dixiecrats, as they were called, insisted their campaign was not about equal rights but about the dangers of a big government with centralized powers in Washington, D.C. Governor Fielding said "This is not a fourth party. I say to you that we are the true Democrats of the Southland and these United States." This idea of a satellite group was something new on the political scene. Satellite groups were stronger than a pressure group but weaker than a full-fledged party.

Although the Dixiecrats knew they could never win the election, they hoped to throw the election into the lap of the House of Representatives. This never happened. Many Democratic political leaders from the South simply swallowed their pride and stayed with the major party.

As with the Bull Moose and LaFollette progressives, the Dixiecrats failed to build a solid base for their party. States with large populations required large numbers of signatures on petitions and nominating papers. This called for strong local organizations, which was lacking. Truman survived this three-prong attack—from Wallace, Thurmond, and Republican contender Thomas Dewey—and won the election.

The full impact of the separation of the Dixiecrats came following the election, when many defected to the Republican party. Strom Thurmond was one of the first to do this. He won every election he entered as a Republican and served in Congress for many years.

American Independent Party

The late 1960s were years of great distress and turbulence in the nation. Civil rights protests and Vietnam War protests were rampant in the land, causing fear and unrest. Out of this chaotic time came a voice from the South that said government bureaucrats were "pointy head" intellectuals. This was the voice of George Wallace, the governor of Alabama. Wallace launched a new party that he called the American Independent party. Its slogan was "All Power to the People."

George Wallace became well-known in 1963 when, as governor, he blocked the doorway to the University of Alabama, barring two black students from entering. After this act drew nationwide attention, Americans who opposed segregation identified with Wallace. Encouraged by this new popularity, he entered the Democratic primaries in 1964 just to measure the response. Despite lack of funding and little organization, Wallace received support above what anyone expected.

Wallace appealed not only to racists but to every American who feared change. He focused on law and order, running your own schools, and protecting property rights. When Wallace announced he was going to run on a separate ticket, support for him swelled to new numbers. Because Wallace knew that ballot access was the biggest barrier for third-party candidates, he hired four lawyers to work on this project alone. The lawyers worked hard and eventually Wallace's name was on ballots in 50 states. His name wound up on Ohio's ballot only because the U.S. Supreme Court overruled a state access law regarding signing of petitions. This was a historical achievement for a third-party candidate. He was, however, unable to make it on the ballot of the District of Columbia.

Meanwhile, the two major party candidates, Democrat Hubert Humphrey and Republican Richard Nixon, warned the nation that a vote for George Wallace would be a wasted vote. Nixon especially worked hard to undermine the Wallace votes by creating a Southern strategy. The Republicans promised to go easy on school desegregation and to get tough on crime. This took back many Southern votes that Wallace might have received.

Nevertheless, Wallace won nearly 10 million votes. This amounted to more votes than any other third-party candidate had received up to that time. In 1972 Wallace returned to the Democratic party, and the American Independent party nominated yet another candidate. Without the outspoken Wallace as their leader, the party weakened and then disappeared.

While again campaigning for president under the banner of the Democrats, George Wallace was shot by an assassin and left paralyzed from the waist down. He spent the rest of his life in a wheel chair.

A True Independent

Few Americans had ever heard of Representative John Anderson from Illinois when he ran for president in 1980. The white-haired Anderson at first ran as a liberal Republican. Early in his career, Anderson was one of the most conservative members of the House of Representatives. He actively fought against many of President Kennedy's social reform issues. Later he changed his views. He protested the nuclear weapons race against the Soviet Union and took a stand for stronger gun control. Because he did most of his work in Congress rather than in front of the media, few people had ever heard his name.

In 1979 he was about to retire from more than 20 years in Congress when he made the decision to run for president on the Republican ticket. By April of 1980 Ronald Reagan had captured enough convention delegates in the primaries to become the Republican candidate, cutting off Anderson's chances. Anderson remained in the race as an independent candidate. He dubbed his movement the National Unity Campaign. There was no organized party, and there was no convention. His sole purpose seemed to be to give voters another choice.

He shunned political labels but was determined to run as the "ideas candidate." He enjoyed putting forth unpopular plans that he was convinced the country needed. He proposed a fifty cent per gallon tax on gasoline, which would be balanced by a fifty percent cut in Social Security taxes.

Representative John Anderson during his 1980 campaign for the presidency. Like all third-party candidates, Anderson brought forward controversial issues, such as a gasoline tax, that the major parties avoided.

Anderson had no emotional campaign issues, such as those held by former third-party candidates—for example, the abolition of slavery, free silver, or states' rights. He didn't rail against the current president, as Teddy Roosevelt had done. His surprising popularity was mostly the result of voter dissatisfaction with the two candidates: incumbent president Jimmy Carter and Republican nominee Ronald Reagan. By late spring the polls were showing he had the support of 20 percent of the voters.

In spite of this support, as with all third-party candidates, the odds were against him. He was forced to spend a great deal of time raising money and fulfilling the requirements to get his name on the ballots. When it came time for the presidential debates, President Carter refused to enter into a debate with Anderson, which weakened the latter's credibility. Anderson did, however, enter into a televised debate with Reagan.

Another drawback was trying to find a well-known leader to run as his vice president. He finally chose Democrat Patrick Lucey, a retired governor of Wisconsin and former ambassador to Mexico. If few people knew of Anderson, fewer still had ever heard of Lucey.

As the election neared, Anderson's support faltered. In the end the most he achieved was to provide an alternative to about six million voters who were dissatisfied with the choices of the major party's candidates.

Twelve years later voter dissatisfaction fueled the campaign of the most recent in the long line of third-party candidates, H. Ross Perot. Perot proved that Americans were not only disappointed in candidates, they were in an antigovernment frame of mind. Sentiment ran high as Perot's popularity grew.

Some say that were it not for the Federal Election Campaign Act, which bestows millions of federal dollars on the two major parties, third-party candidates like Perot would be much more of a threat. FECA not only limits federal funds, it also limits private gifts. This means that future successful third-party candidates may have to be incredibly wealthy people like Perot.

Summary

The media has changed the face of politics in the 20th century. Public relations managers and image consultants are ready for hire. Instead of building an image over a series of elections, today's candidates can purchase the advice and expertise needed for quick and effective exposure. With the availability of computers, telephones, postage meters, direct mail, and expert consultants, candidates don't feel the need for local party organization as they had in previous years.

Aside from these new innovations, we find that even the most recent third-party candidates continue to face insurmountable odds in their campaigns. As mentioned, these include difficult ballot access laws, lack of funds, and lack of media coverage.

The biggest deterrent to the success of third-party candidates in the United States continues to be the strength of the two-party system. Voters may express frustration and dissatisfaction, but most are still extremely loyal to their party. Compromise within party ranks usually keeps the disgruntled members from splitting off.

In the midst of it all, third parties continue to bring forth controversial issues that no major party will touch. They give those issues greater visibility. Third-party candidates emerge as a release valve for a people who have proven over and over that they delight in having a variety of choices—even in their politics.

Glossary

Abolitionist—A person who believes slavery should be abolished.

Campaign—An organized activity to gain a political goal or office.

Candidate—A person who seeks or is nominated for an office.

Factions—Internal discord or conflicting subgroups within an organization or group.

Fusion—The joining of two or more groups or parties to support a common candidate or common program.

Monopolies—A company or group having total control over a commercial activity.

Nominee—A person chosen as a candidate for an election or an office.

Party slate—The list of names allowed on a voting ballot.

Party platform—A formal declaration of principles by a political party or a candidate.

Political convention—The gathering of a political party for the purpose of choosing candidates for president and vice president.

Suffrage—The right, privilege, or act of voting.

Third party—Any political party that forms outside of and independent from the two major political parties.

Further Reading

Bredeson, Carmen. *Ross Perot: Billionaire Politician.* Springfield, NJ: Enslow Publishers, 1995.

Haskins, James, and Kathleen Benson. *Bound for America: The Forced Migration of Africans to the New World.* NY: Lothrop, Lee & Shepard Books, 1999.

Henry, Christopher E. *The Electoral College.* NY: Franklin Watts, 1996.

Kendall, Martha E. *Susan B. Anthony: Voice for Women's Voting Rights.* Springfield, NJ: Enslow Publishers, 1997.

Maestro, Betsy. *The Voice of the People: American Democracy in Action.* NY: Lothrop, Lee & Shepard Books, 1996.

Quiri, Patricia Ryan. *The Bill of Rights.* Chicago: Children's Press, 1999.

Quiri, Patricia Ryan. *Congress.* Chicago: Children's Press, 1999.

Sher, Linda. *The Vote: Making Your Voice Heard.* Austin, TX: Raintree Steck-Vaughn, 1993.

Index

ABOUT THE AUTHOR: Norma Jean Lutz, who lives in Tulsa, Oklahoma, has been writing professionally since 1977. She is the author of more than 250 short stories and articles as well as 36 fiction and nonfiction books. Of all the writing she does, she most enjoys writing children's books.

SENIOR CONSULTING EDITOR Arthur M. Schlesinger, jr. is the leading American historian of our time. He won the Pulitzer Prize for his book *The Age of Jackson* (1945) and again for *A Thousand Days* (1965). This chronicle of the Kennedy Administration also won a National Book Award. Professor Schlesinger is the Albert Schweitzer Professor of the Humanities at the City University of New York, and has been involved in several other Chelsea House projects, including the REVOLUTIONARY WAR LEADERS and COLONIAL LEADERS series.

Picture Credits

page
8: Reuters/Robert Girox/ Archive Photos
12: Reuters/Mark Cardwell/ Archive Photos
13: Archive Photos
14: Reuters/Scott Cohen/ Archive Photos
16: Santi Visalli/ Archive Photos
18: Archive Photos
20: Blank Achives/ Archive Photos
24: Archive Photos
27: Archive Photos
29: Archive Photos
31: Museum of the City of New York/ Archive Photos
32: Archive Photos
35: Archive Photos
38: Archive Photos
40: AP/Wide World Photos
42: Archive Photos
47: New York Times Co./ Archive Photos
49: American Stock/ Archive Photos
50: AP/Wide World Photos
52: APA/Archive Photos
53: Archive Photos
54: Richardo Watson/ Archive Photos
58: Bernard Gotfryd/ Archive Photos